THE ARMOUR AND ARMS OF HENRY VIII

Thom Richardson

CONTENTS

Front cover: The 1540
armour. II.8

Page 1: The 'horned
helmet'. IV.22

Page 2: Gun shield,
partizan, spear and
'Henry VIII's Walking Staff'.
V.79, VII.147, VII.4, XIV.1

Back cover: The Foot
Combat armour. II.6

FOREWORD

The history of England records no more charismatic figure than King Henry VIII. From his athletic youth to his premature, indulgence-induced decline, he appeared a colossus to his contemporaries and succeeding generations have largely agreed with this assessment. His personality and achievements loom large over the history of our country, the Tower of London and especially the Royal Armouries.

His reign may seem a curious amalgam of the old and the new, but during it the Kingdom of England emerged as a power to be reckoned with. Henry took what he needed from the past, for instance by using the mystique of the mythic English King Arthur in his dealings with the Hapsburg Emperor, Charles V. But he quickly discarded what he did not need, for instance ridding his arsenal of almost everything antique in order to re-equip with the modern weapons befitting a great renaissance prince. He fitted out his fleet with the most modern weapons, including artillery whose formidable firepower is only now coming to be fully recognised. But at the same time he retained the long bow as a military weapon and made vain but continued efforts to make his subjects practise regularly with this traditional weapon. Perhaps it is these apparent inconsistencies that make him such a perpetually fascinating figure.

Here was a King of England with a real fascination for weapons and armour, someone who took a personal interest in their manufacture and design. He was the founder of the only English royal armour-making workshop, situated at his palace at Greenwich, a workshop still to yield up its secrets – a recent archaeological dig has failed to find it where it should have been. Henry was no great warrior though he did take part in two foreign campaigns. But he was a lifelong sportsman, in his youth devoted to tilting, foot combat, wrestling and archery, while in his later years preferring the more sedate, though still active, sport of falconry. Twice, in 1524 and 1536, his love of jousting brought him within inches of death – even for kings it was a dangerous sport.

Henry's impact upon the Royal Armouries and its collections was immense. The arms and armour made for him, his personal guard and his army still form the core of the collection we hold in trust for the nation. He and they are endlessly fascinating as readers of this book will discover for themselves.

Guy Wilson
Master of the Armouries 1988–2002

INTRODUCTION

Henry VIII ruled England at a time of profound change. Before his reign England was an isolated medieval kingdom, which had just suffered a civil war and had lost the long war with France, along with most of its possessions on the mainland. After his reign England emerged as a mainstream Renaissance European power, involved in Continental diplomacy and events, with its own new Church at loggerheads with the Pope and the Catholic Church. The events which brought about this sea-change in English history are closely involved with the King himself and his personal actions and ambitions.

It was under Henry VIII that the English army was transformed from a medieval army of infantry archers and billmen to a 'modern' army armed with firearms and pikes. The nascent collections at the Tower reflect that change. All the medieval arms stored there were scrapped, and can now be understood only through inventories. New arms were largely imported from the Continent, and these form the beginnings of the massive arsenal that survives to the present as the Royal Armouries' collection.

Henry was the son of Henry Tudor, Henry VII of England, whose victory over Richard III at the battle of Bosworth Field in 1485 and marriage to Elizabeth of York brought to an end the bloodiest series of conflicts on English soil and established a new dynasty. Prince Henry was born on 28 June 1491, and became heir to the throne on the death of his elder brother Arthur in 1502. In 1507 at the age of 15 he attended his first tournament, and a year later spent day after day at Richmond tilting. He remained a tournament enthusiast for the remainder of his adult life. On 21 April 1509 Henry VII died after a long illness, and Prince Henry inherited the throne of England at the age of 17. He was crowned in June, and in the same month finally, after years of fruitless negotiation between his father, the Pope and her parents, Ferdinand and Isabella of Castile and Aragon, married his brother's widow, Katherine of Aragon. At the great tournament at Westminster in February 1511, in which Henry tilted as 'Coeur Loyal' (meaning 'loyal heart'), the combined initials of the young king and his somewhat older queen, H and K, featured largely in the lavish decorations.

◀ **Portrait of Henry VIII after Holbein**

Oil on panel, English, late 16th century. I.51

Arms and armour had been made in England throughout the Middle Ages. The London guild of armourers, for example, which survives to this day as the Worshipful Company of Armourers and Brasiers, evolved from the Guild of Heaumers (helmet-makers) in the 14th century. It received its Royal Charter in 1453 and continued to make armour until the end of the 17th century. Unfortunately it is not currently possible to identify their works with any certainty. Two groups of helms, one of the late 14th century and another of the early 15th, are almost certainly of English manufacture, but few other pieces can be identified. Certainly by the middle of the 15th century the nobility of England bought armour from abroad, occasionally from Italy, where Milan was recognized as the leading production centre, but mostly from Flanders, where many Milanese had migrated to take advantage of the market in north-west Europe. A model armour, on a wooden equestrian sculpture of St George subduing a lizard-like dragon, is preserved in the hall of the Armourers and Brasiers Company.

It is quite clear that English production was not up to the standard of the Flemish (or Italian or Austrian) craftsmen, and it is clear that Henry wished to have his own armour workshop, just like Holy Roman Emperor Maximilian I (1459 – 1519). Accordingly from 1511 Henry made several attempts to set up workshops, in Southwark and Greenwich. Both these locations are south of the river Thames and hence outside the City of London where the London Companies and craft guilds held sway. Maximilian did the

▼ Henry VIII tilting, at the great tournament at Westminster in February 1511. College of Arms, the Westminster Tournament Roll.

Reproduced by permission of the Kings, Heralds and Pursuivants of Arms

same thing when he set up Konrad Seusenhofer (originally from Augsburg) in Innsbruck, close to but outside the control of the Innsbruck armourers, who, based in Mulhau, were very unhappy about the arrangement but were unable to do anything about it. The early experiment with the Milanese, including Filippo de Grampis and Giovanni Angelo de Littis who were working there from 1512, did not prove long-lasting as they were gone by about 1515. But the Flemings and Germans were to prove more permanent.

Model of St George slaying the dragon

In steel on a wooden figure, presented to the Armourers' Company of London in 1527 and probably made by William Vynyard (alias Segar), Master of the Company.

In the collection of the Worshipful Company of Armourers and Brasiers

Henry's first foreign enterprise, alliance with the Holy Roman Emperor Maximilian I (reigned 1493–1519) against the French, culminated in victory in the battle of the Spurs (named after the rapidity of the French knights in retreat) on 16 August 1513. They met before the battle 'in the fowlest wether that lightly have been seen since' and formed a cordial understanding. Maximilian himself with thirty of his men-at-arms took part in the battle. The victim of the battle was the town of Tournoi, into which Henry rode in triumph. Beside him rode his nephew the young Archduke Charles, later Charles V of Spain. Naturally Henry immediately held a tournament there, in the market square, taking up all the paving slabs for the purpose.

◄ Detail of the 'horned helmet'. IV.22

► Maximilian I and Henry VIII at the battle of the Spurs, from *Der Weiss Kunig*, 1514, illustrated by Hans Burgkmair (1473–1531).

© Royal Armouries

THE 'HORNED HELMET'

Meanwhile Maximilian was preparing a diplomatic gift that was to change the course of armour making in England. In 1511 he commissioned his court armourer at Innsbruck, Konrad Seusenhofer, to make an armour for Henry. After the usual delays and wrangling over expenses, the armour was delivered in 1514, together with another armour that Henry had commissioned privately. All that remains of this magnificent armour is the famous helmet with ram's horns and spectacles. However Seusenhofer manufactured at the same time a similar harness (armour) for Henry's companion at the triumph at Tournoi, the Archduke Charles V, and this armour survives in the Kunsthistorisches Museum in Vienna. Comparison between the two shows that Henry's armour too was decorated with the same silver gilt fretted panels laid over velvet which survive on Charles' armour, as well as being etched with further decoration and partially gilt. The main part of the armour is identifiable from the 1547 inventory of Henry's possessions in the first house at Greenwich as the 'Harnesse given unto the kings Majestie by Themperor Maximilian wth a base of stele and goldesmythe worke Silver and guilte with A border abowt the same silver and guilte of Goldesmythes work'.

Armour of the future Charles V

Made by Konrad Seusenhofer, Austrian, Innsbruck, 1512–14.
KHM-Museumsverband, Vienna A109

The 'horned helmet'

An armet originally forming part of an armour presented to King Henry VIII by the Emperor Maximilian I, made by Konrad Seusenhofer, Austrian, Innsbruck, 1512–14. IV.22

Detail of etched decoration on the cheekpiece.

The helmet was separated even at this time, for it was with a 'playne harness' on the third horse in the second house at Greenwich, 'a hedde pece wt a Rammes horne silver pcell guilte.' The remainder of the armour was apparently sold off as scrap in 1649 at the end of the English Civil Wars and the establishment of the Commonwealth. The surviving helmet escaped this fate, being kept on a separate stand (the armour clearly had alternative helmets) and was used in 17th-century displays at the Tower of London as part of the 'armour of Will Somers', Henry VIII's court jester. One hundred and fifty years after its manufacture its original ownership had been completely forgotten.

In more recent years huge academic arguments have raged over the authenticity of the helmet. Whether, for example, the ram's horns and spectacles were originally part of it, or added later. Current research indicates that its form was an allusion to the popular *Ship of Fools* by Sebastian Brant, an in-joke shared between Maximilian and Henry.

▲ An armourer's workshop in the early 16th century: Maximilian I visits his armourer Konrad Seusenhofer, from *Der Weiss Kunig*, 1514, illustrated by Hans Burgkmair (1473–1531).

© Royal Armouries

ARMET

No firm evidence regarding the other armour Henry purchased from Konrad Seusenhofer is known. However one of the most beautiful armets known survived in the Rotunda Museum at Woolwich, and probably came from the Tower, though it cannot be traced in the archives (mainly because the records of the collection in the 18th and early 19th century are largely lost). It is clearly made at Innsbruck, and can be attributed to Konrad Seusenhofer. It is etched with Tudor roses around the lining rivets that surround its lower edge, and physically fits other elements of Henry's head defences. It is possible that this helmet is part of the armour commissioned from Konrad Seusenhofer by the King.

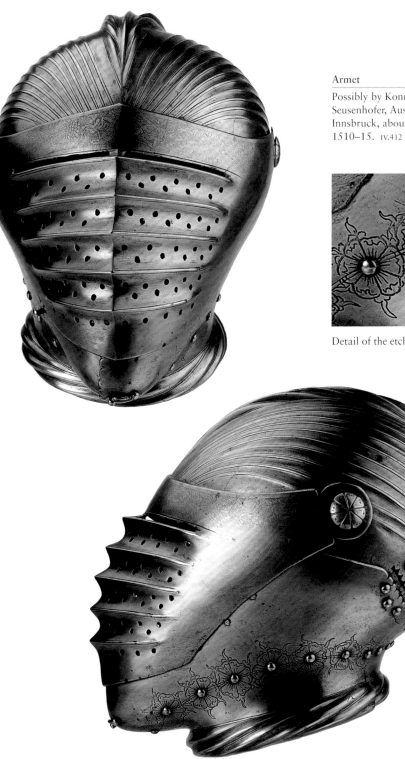

Armet

Possibly by Konrad
Seusenhofer, Austrian,
Innsbruck, about
1510–15. IV.412

Detail of the etched Tudor roses.

HORSE ARMOUR

The Innsbruck workshop does not seem to have been commissioned to make the horse armour or bard intended to go with Maximilian's gift armour. Instead this task was entrusted to one of Maximilian's armourers in Flanders, probably Guillem Margot. Unlike the armour for Henry's person, the horse armour is decorated with embossing as well as engraving and gilding. The decoration features the firesteels and crosses raguly (an heraldic term for crosses

Horse armour of King Henry VIII

Probably by Guillem Margot, presented by Maximilian I, Flemish, about 1510. VI.6-12

made of rough branches) of the Order of the Golden Fleece, with which Henry was awarded in 1505, and the pomegranate badges of his wife Katherine. The saddle steels, the pommel and cantle, are decorated to match the main parts of the bard, the shaffron, peytral, flanchards and crupper. Even the plates for the reins, fretted with the same badges, survive. Only the crinet is not embossed, though it has a similar engraved border of firesteels and pomegranates, and this may be the only surviving part of another of Henry's bards. The decoration of the bard is attributed to another Fleming, Paul van Vrelant. The bard was still with Maximilian's gift armour at Greenwich in the 1547 inventory, 'A barde of stele wth the Burgonion Crosse and the fusye (fire steel)'.

Detail from the rein plates, including a firesteel and pomegranates.

THE 'SILVERED AND ENGRAVED' ARMOUR

The first known product of Henry's new workshop is the famous 'Silvered and Engraved' armour, made about 1515. The armour is silvered overall and formerly gilt, and engraved through the silvering. The decoration commemorates the marriage of Henry VIII and Katherine. On the breastplate is a figure of St George and on the backplate one of St Barbara; these match the decoration of the horse armour, whose decoration includes scenes from the lives of these Saints. The rest of the armour is decorated with an all-over pattern of scrolling vegetation including Tudor roses and the pomegranates of Aragon. On the back of each greave is a female figure emerging from the calyx of a flower; the neck-band of the figure on the left greave is inscribed GLVCK. The wings of the poleyns bear the sheaf of arrows badge of Ferdinand II of Aragon and the combined rose and pomegranate badge of Katherine of Aragon, while the toecaps of the sabatons have the castle badge of Castile and the Tudor portcullis.

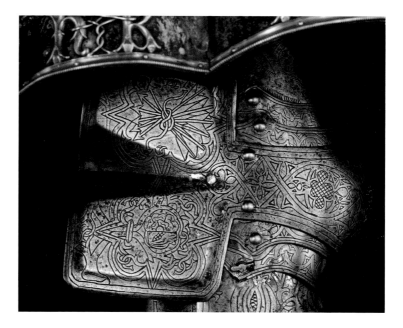

◄ The 'Silvered and Engraved' armour of King Henry VIII. II.5

▶ Detail on the wing of the right poleyn.

The base or skirt is bordered by intertwined letters H and K for Henry and Katherine. The maker's mark stamped on the back of the skull, a crowned helmet, is similar to the mark used by Peter Fevers, one of the Flemings. On the bard is the M and crescent mark of Guillem Margot. The decoration is the work of Paul van Vrelant of Brussels, who held the appointment of the King's 'harness gilder' from 1514 until at least 1520. Clearly Henry recruited craftsmen who had been working for Maximilian in Flanders for his new armour workshop.

▶ The 'Silvered and Engraved' armour shown dismounted.

Maker's mark on the helmet.

One of the pairs of initials of Henry and Katherine on the hem of the skirt.

Detail showing the martyrdom of St George on the crupper of the horse armour.

The 'Silvered and Engraved'
armour of King Henry VIII

Decorated by Paul van
Vrelant, English, Greenwich.
Horse armour probably
Flemish by Martin van
Royne, about 1515.
II.5, VI.1–5

HORSE ARMOUR

By 1515 Henry had a workshop staffed with eleven German and Flemish armourers, collectively termed Almains. From late 1515, or early 1516, the workshop was moved from Greenwich to Southwark while improvements were made to the facilities at Greenwich. There they stayed for at least six years before returning to Greenwich.

This bard, which Mann dated about 1530, comprises a peytral, crupper, one flanchard and a pair of stirrups. The crinet formerly displayed with is was a modern restoration and the shaffron associated, while the saddle and steels are original but associated, as their decoration does not match. It is decorated with sprays of embossed flutes and bands of etched and gilt foliage on a hatched ground, with the king's badges, the rose and portcullis, repeated at intervals. It is on account of the 'Italianate' nature of its decoration that the bard is associated with the Italian craftsmen working for the king.

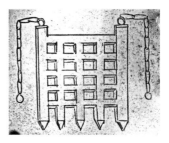

The portcullis, one of Henry's badges, from the Italian bard.

▼ Horse armour

Probably by the Italians, Greenwich or Southwark, about 1515. VI.14–16

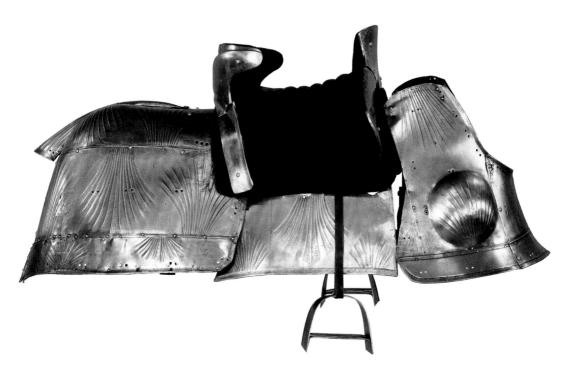

The accession of François I to the throne of France brought a change to the diplomatic relations between the two countries. The new entente was embodied in the great tournament, the *Champ de Drap d'Or* or Field of Cloth of Gold, held between Calais and Guisnes, on the border of the two realms, in 1520. The tournament would culminate in the signing of a peace treaty between the two powers, as well as giving the two young kings ample opportunity to show off their chivalric skill. Complex negotiations preceded the event, and in the course of these a small but critical change in the rules for the armour worn in the foot combat event, in which François and Henry would fight in the same team, occurred.

◀ The Foot Combat armour of King Henry VIII. II.6

▼ Detail from *The Field of Cloth of Gold*, painted about 1545, artist unknown.

Royal Collection Trust/© Her Majesty Queen Elizabeth II 2015

FOOT COMBAT ARMOUR

Henry's new armourers were working away on the armour known now as the 'Foot Combat' armour of Henry VIII when tragedy struck. The original armour specified for the foot combat was 'field armour with pieces of advantage … with an armet without … helm, demi-helm nor basnet'. Some three months before the event, a different type of armour was specified for the event. Henry's agent in France, Sir Richard Wingfield, wrote on 16 March 'as touchyng the combatt at the barrier, ther is left out these words ffollowing "with pieces of advantage". And in stede thereof is sett "in Tonnelett and bacinett."'

Work on the extraordinary Foot Combat armour ceased, and it remained unfinished and undecorated. In the 17th century the armour was still 'rough from the hammer' and though centuries of polishing by soldiers at the Tower with brick dust and Rangoon oil have made it bright today, one small portion of the gorget, hidden below the breastplate to which it is bolted, preserves the original surface. The armour is technically quite remarkable. It has many features that were to become characteristic of Greenwich production (such as the upward-overlapping pauldron lames) and others that were highly unusual. These include sets of articulating lames inside all the joints of the body, contrived to enable all the limbs to move while protecting every possible aperture. Though other similar armours exist, the Foot Combat armour is one of the most remarkable examples of this type of armourers' work surviving.

Detail of gauntlets.

Detail of 'bear's paw' type articulated sabatons.

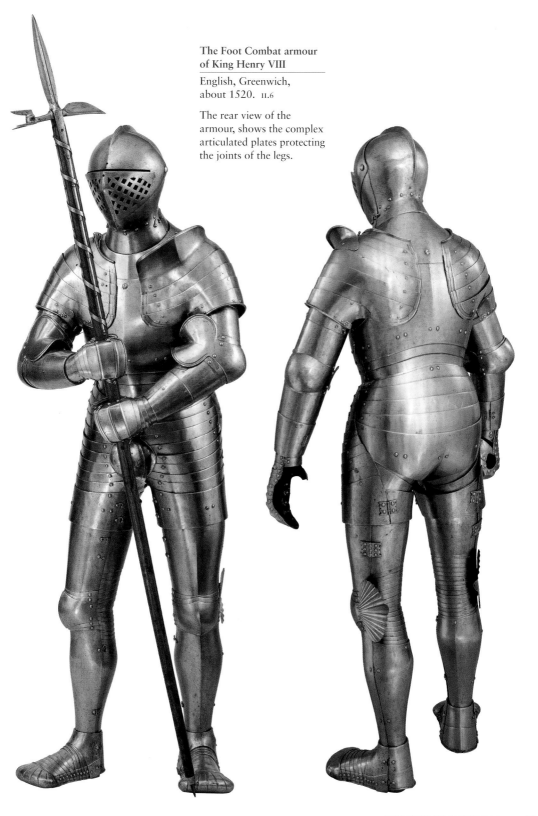

**The Foot Combat armour
of King Henry VIII**

English, Greenwich,
about 1520. II.6

The rear view of the
armour, shows the complex
articulated plates protecting
the joints of the legs.

TONLET ARMOUR

The armourers at Greenwich now had a very short time to make ready a new armour for the King to wear at the Field of Cloth of Gold. They succeeded in preparing an armour, now known as the Tonlet armour of King Henry VIII, by adapting a number of existing pieces, manufacturing additional pieces from new, and decorating the armour. The armour has a great bacinet, the type of helmet traditionally used in the foot combat, originally made in Milan (marks of the Missaglia workshop of that city appear on the rear of the skull) but with a modified visor. The vambraces and leg defences were also adapted from existing field armours. The vambraces have the narrow articulated lames protecting the insides of the elbow joints characteristic of foot combat armours added, while the greaves of the leg defences have slots for the attachment of spurs, essential for a field harness but quite unnecessary for a foot combat armour. Only the pauldrons, which are of the characteristic Greenwich type with upward-overlapping plates, and the hooped skirt or tonlet, were made new. The etched decoration retains traces of gilding. The decoration includes figures of St George, the Virgin and Child, Tudor roses, the collar of the Order of the Garter and, around the top of the left greave, the garter itself. The armour survived in the palace at Greenwich until 1649 when it was transferred to the Tower. The leg defences, however, escaped, and were reunited with the rest of the armour in 1947, having been in the collection of the Dymoke family, the hereditary Royal Champions, at Scrivelsby.

◄ The Order of the Garter etched on the left greave.

The figure of the Virgin and Child etched on the bacinet.

The Tonlet armour of King Henry VIII

English, Greenwich, 1520. II.7

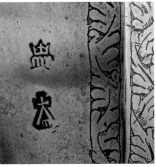

Detail of maker's marks on the skull of the bacinet.

The Tournament

The 'field' at the Field of Cloth of Gold was 900 x 320 ft (274 x 82 m), and was dominated by the 'tree of honour'. This was an artificial tree made of pine branches and covered in green damask and cloth of gold some 10 m high, standing on an artificial mountain or *perron*, in the form of a conjoined hawthorn for England and a raspberry for France (called the Aubespine and Framboisier). On this were hung three shields, black and silver for the tilt, gold and tawny for the tourney and silver for the foot combat. The challengers or 'comers' touched the shields for the events in which they wished to compete, and the heralds recorded their challenges on plaques hung below the shields, and placed their armorial shields around the base of the 'mountain'. Grandstands were set at either side of the field, and it was surrounded by a deep ditch. The English as hosts were responsible for all the provisions of the tournament, and the large quantity of arms (lance heads, vamplates, swords etc.) is recorded. The preparations included the transport of a mill from the Almain workshop at Greenwich to Guisnes, and the attendance of some 26 armourers including one 'Assamus', presumably Erasmus Kyrkenar who was to succeed Martin van Royne as Master before 1540.

◀ The Tonlet armour of King Henry VIII. II.7

▼ Portrait of François I (1494-1547), 1538, by Titian (Tiziano Vecellio) (about 1488 – 1576).
© Louvre, Paris, France/ Bridgeman Images

The first six days of competition were jousts, which lasted from Monday 11 June to Tuesday 19 June. On each day eight courses were held, starting after lunch at 1 o'clock and finishing at 6. The two kings competed in the same team or band on four of these days. On Wednesday 20 and Thursday 21 June tourneys were held, between bands of 10–13 men-at-arms, using lances and single-handed swords. On the last of these days one of the bands of challengers was headed by Robert III de la Marck, Maréchal de Fleuranges, the hero of the battle of Novara (where he is said to have received 46 wounds) in the Italian Wars. Henry fought with Fleuranges with such vigour that he 'bare back M Florenges and brake his Poldron (shoulder defence) and him disarmed'.

Finally came the days of foot combats at the barriers, on Friday 22 and Saturday 23 June. The first round of combat was with 'Punchion spears' and single-handed swords, which were given to the combatants when the spears were 'spent'. In these events the 'two valyaunte kynges' fought 'with such force that the fier sprang out of their armure'. The second round of combats were with throwing spears ('casting dartes') and two-handed swords. The kings competed on both days, the second of which was followed by a masque, and brought the tournament to a close. Despite the best efforts of his panegyrist Edward Hall, it is clear that Henry did not do particularly well at the tournament, though he won the archery competition. He was humiliated in the wrestling, which was held on Wednesday 13 June. Henry asked to wrestle François, and was given a '*tour de Bretagne*' (a clever hold now sadly unidentifiable) and a 'Marvellous fall' for his pains.

THE FLEURANGES ARMOUR

A Greenwich field armour made between 1520 and 1525, now in the collection of the Musée de l'Armée in Paris, is thought to have been presented by Henry to Fleuranges to commemorate this event.

The Fleuranges armour

Greenwich, about 1525.

Musée de l'Armée, Paris. G46, H47

At the jousts held on Shrove Tuesday (6 March) in 1527 Henry appeared in a 'newe harness all gilte of a strange fashion that had not bene sene'. His team, wearing cloth of gold embroidered with knots of silver, tilted before the French ambassadors with a team of nine led by Henry Courtenay, Marquess of Exeter in blue velvet and white satin 'like the waves of the sea'. On 5 May that year another party of ambassadors from France, led by François II de la Tour d'Auvergne, Viscomte de Turenne, were entertained with jousts and an elaborate masque on the theme of the combined joy of the English and French peoples at the peace between their nations, in the form of the Alliance of Amiens, signed on 30 April of that year. Turenne and Henry both took part in the masque, and the ambassadors departed bearing 'greate rewards'. Among these seems to have been the armour worn by Henry at the Shrove Tuesday jousts.

THE 'GENOUILHAC' ARMOUR

The armour, if this identification is correct, survives in the collection of the Metropolitan Museum of Art in New York. It is dated 1527 in no less than five places, and is etched and gilt overall. The themes of the decoration include on the leg defences the labours of Hercules, and on the upper half a merknight and mermaid, supplemented with elephants and castles, and various putti and animals. The decoration has been argued to have been executed by the Florentine artist Giovanni da Maiano, who produced a similar scheme at Hampton Court, or Hans Holbein, who is first recorded working for the King during his first stay in England in 1526–8 (or possibly both, since two hands seem to be responsible for the two types of decoration).

The armour was made by the Almains under Martin van Royne at Greenwich. It includes a locking gauntlet for the tourney, and had a set of reinforces for the tilt, as its manifer survives though its grandguard and pasguard do not. It also includes saddle steels and the shaffron and crinet from its bard, but whether or not it had the other parts of the bard is unknown. It has the first example of a feature now unique to the Greenwich workshop. This is an inner breastplate or ventral plate strapped to the body and designed to lift the weight of the cuirass and arm defences from the shoulders by means of the central bolt to which the breastplate and plackart were secured. It is recorded that François I in 1520 disclosed this secret device to Henry, offering his armourers to make one for Henry if he sent one of his arming doublets for a pattern. If this was indeed made for Henry VIII, it is interesting to note that his waist measurement was a good deal less than 40 inches. The armour was purchased directly from the French family of Crussol, Ducs d'Uzes, and it now bears a modern escutcheon with the arms of Jacques de Genouilhac, known as Galiot, Grand Master of the Artillery under François I, a relative of Turenne and ancestor of the Crussols.

DIVORCE AND REMARRIAGE

A fragment of a plain Greenwich armour, a plate sabaton, made for Henry VIII at about the same time survives in the Royal Armouries' collection, but from this time until much later in Henry's life few pieces survive. He also does not seem to have participated in the tournaments that had been such a part of his life hitherto. This may be explained by the events of the King's life during that period. His affair with Anne Boleyn began around 1526, and the first steps towards nullity of his marriage of 18 years to Katherine of Aragon were taken in 1527. Meanwhile the Peace of Cambrai was signed between Charles V and François I in 1529, bringing a generation of conflict to a temporary close. On 25 January 1533 he married Anne Boleyn in secret, and by 11 July Pope Clement VII had excommunicated him from the Catholic Church. On 3 November Parliament proclaimed Henry head of the Church of England. It is interesting that the King does not appear to have taken part in any jousts after 1527, and the May Day jousts of 1534 are the only ones he is recorded as even attending (if only to leave early). Perhaps the King was, after reaching the age of 36, getting too old for the tournament, but it is noteworthy that, if the identification of the Genouilhac armour as his is correct, he had certainly not attained the great girth that his later armours attest.

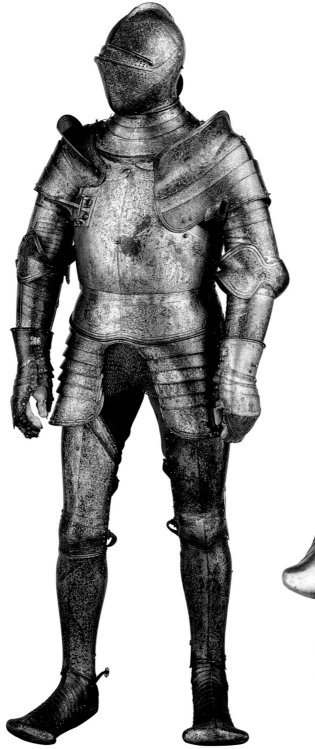

◀ The Genouilhac armour

Probably originally
made for Henry VIII,
Greenwich, dated 1527.

The Metropolitan Museum of Art,
New York. William H Riggs Gift and
Rogers Fund, 1919 (19.131.1,2)

© 2015 The Metropolitan Museum
of Art/Art Resource/Scala, Florence

▲ Sabaton

From a plain Greenwich
armour of Henry VIII,
about 1527. II.8T

Henry had, of course, his first daughter Mary, born to Katherine in 1516, and his second daughter Elizabeth born to Anne Boleyn in 1533. However, the increasingly desperate quest for a male heir seems to have obsessed him during the latter stages of his life, and this combined with the increasingly Byzantine intrigues at his court to produce the rapid succession of marriages for which Henry, however unjustly, is remembered.

Anne's unfortunate miscarriage in January 1536 seems to have coincided with Henry's serious injury in a tournament. By 19 May Anne had been arrested for high treason and executed, and Henry was married to Jane Seymour on 30 May. The future Edward VI was born at Hampton Court on 12 October 1537, but Jane never recovered from the birth and died on 24 October. Henry appears to have felt a deep sense of loss at her death; he wore mourning for some time afterwards, and fell ill with a fistula on his leg. His time remained occupied with religious problems, and outbreaks of unrest in the country such as the 'Pilgrimage of Grace'. By 1539 following a spate of executions his health was recovered enough to seek another bride. He married Anne of Cleves on 24 September 1539 but the marriage was not a success, and was nullified by parliament on 9 July of the following year.

ARMOUR

◀ **Gun shield**

Of the group with upper guns from the armoury of Henry VIII. The central panel is etched with a scene featuring Mucius Scaevola. v.39

The few records of the works of his armourers that survive show that they were not idle, despite the lack of royal patronage. Erasmus Kyrkenar's accounts for the year 1536/7, for example, show that they were making a succession of armours to order for the nobility of England, mostly garnitures for the tilt and field with extra pieces at £10–12, and for the field only at £8.

FIREARMS

Though Henry does not seem to have had any new armour made for him during this period, there is evidence of his interest in new firearms technology. By the time of his death in 1547 the inventory of his possessions recorded no fewer than 139 breech-loading guns. Two of them survive from this period of his life, in the Royal Armouries' collection. The first is dated 1537 and stamped 'WH' on top of the breech block, probably by William Hunt, who in 1538 was appointed Keeper of the King's Handguns and Demi-hawks. It was originally fitted with a wheellock mechanism, now lost, and has a breech block hinged at the side so it could be reloaded with a steel cartridge. The gun is decorated with motifs associated with the King, including a crowned Tudor rose supported by lions and the letters 'HR'. It is probably the 'chamber pece in a Stocke of wood, lyned in the cheek with vellet' recorded in the 1547 inventory in the Palace of Westminster.

The maker's initials on top of the breech.

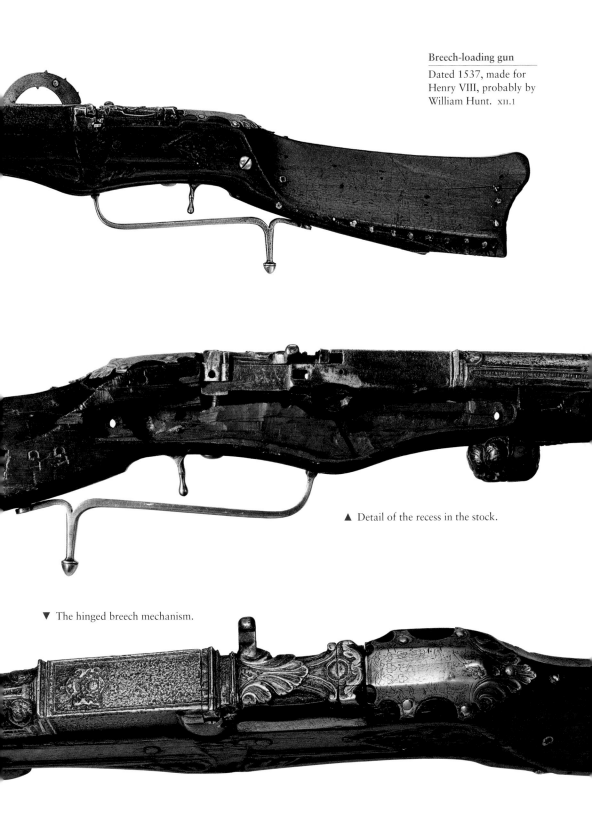

Dated 1537, made for
Henry VIII, probably by
William Hunt. XII.1

▲ Detail of the recess in the stock.

▼ The hinged breech mechanism.

Breech-loading wheellock gun

Made for Henry VIII, German or English, about 1537. XII.2

▼ The breech-block in the open position with an iron cartridge partially withdrawn.

▲ Detail of the muzzle on the left side.

▲ ► A Tudor rose and a fleur-de-lys carved on the left side of the stock.

The second gun is a much larger piece, and again was originally fitted with a wheellock, now lost. It too is breech-loading, with a hinged breech, and one of its reloadable steel cartridges survives. It is probably one of the 'large chamber peces set in Stockes of Walnuttree with fier locks' recorded in the 1547 inventory. This one is neither dated nor stamped with a maker's mark, but may very well be by the same maker as the first. The decoration is also comparable; opposite the lock is carved a Tudor rose, and at the fore-end a fleur-de-lys.

ARTILLERY

Henry's interest in firearms also extended to artillery. An example of a bronze breech-loading cannon in the Royal Armouries' collection illustrates this. The gun has three bores within its rectangular barrel, and slots at the breech for the chambers. It is inscribed HENRICVS OCTAVVS DEI GRACIA ANGLIE ET FRANCIE REX FIDEI DEFENSOR DNS HIBERIE (Henry VIII King of England and France, Defender of the Faith and Lord of Ireland), PETRVS BAVDE GALLVS OPERIS ARTIFEX for the gunmaker, Peter Baude, and has the motto '*pour defendre*' at the muzzle. It is decorated with a crowned Tudor rose supported by putti, and Italianate Renaissance ornament. Baude, a Frenchman by birth, was one of the King's gunfounders and worked at a foundry in Houndsditch, London, with the Owen brothers, perhaps the most famous English gunfounders of the 16th century. Baude is known to have worked with Italian artists Giovanni da Maiano and Bendetto da Rovezzano, who may have introduced the Italian character (the very latest fashion in Renaissance Europe at this time) into the decoration. The gun was in the Mint in the Tower in the inventory of 1540, recorded as 'a square pece of brasse with iij halles and vj chambers', and in the 1547 inventory as a 'Brode fawcons shoting iij shote'. It was unfortunate enough to be in the Grand Storehouse during the great fire of 1841, when it was broken into four pieces and seriously damaged by the fire, and its chambers were lost.

Bronze breech-loading gun
By Peter Baude, English, about 1535. XIX.17

Detail of the decoration on the reinforce.

Inscription at the muzzle.

Detail of the decoration.

GUN SHIELDS

In the inventory of 1547, there were 35 'targetts steilde wt gonnes' brought from Westminster to the Tower, and by 1676 there were 66 in the Tower. The shields may be connected with one of the inventions offered to the King by Giovannibattista di Ravenna in 1544. Alternatively they may be Italian imports fitted with breech-loading guns in England. Sixteen of the gun shields survive in the Royal Armouries' collection. They are of two quite distinct types, those fitted with guns at the centre of the shield, of which there are nine, and those with guns above the centre, of which seven remain.

All the shields are constructed in the form of a cross-ply construction of wooden boards over which steel plates are nailed. The upper-gun group have flat plates, and are mostly decorated with freehand gilt ornament. This decoration incorporates scrolling foliage, but the flat central bosses are etched and gilt with Classical scenes, such as the Roman hero Mucius Scaevola having failed to kill the Etruscan Lars Porsenna, showing his indifference to physical pain by holding his right hand in the fire, or Biblical ones, such as Judith with the head of Holofernes. On the centre-gun group, a small grill for sighting is cut just above the central boss of the shield. Six of these shields have embossed decoration on the plates, while the other three have flat plates gilt with decoration similar to that on the upper-gun group. The guns are all breech-loading, originally with a movable breech containing a rechargeable steel cartridge, and fired by a simple matchlock mechanism. There has been considerable speculation about the intended use of the gun shields, but the discovery of examples on the wreck of the *Mary Rose*, Henry's flagship which sank off Portsmouth in 1540, lends weight to the idea that they were intended for shipboard action. The gun shields were not, of course, personal arms of the King, but are included here because they are closely associated with his personal taste for innovative weapons.

▼ Gun shield

Of the upper-gun group from the armoury of Henry VIII. Back view featuring the mechanism. v.39

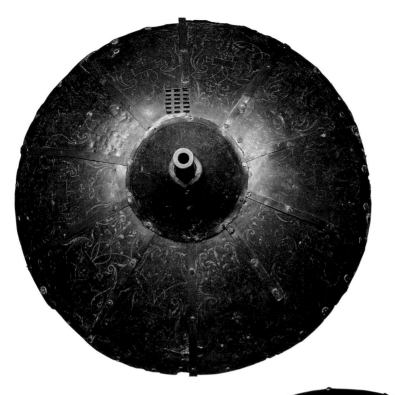

◀ Gun shield

Of the centre-gun group
from the armoury of
Henry VIII. v.79

▶ Gun shield

Of the upper-gun group
from the armoury of
Henry VIII. v.48

STAFF WEAPONS

Another group of weapons not for the personal use of the King but included here as characteristic of his taste are a very extensive group of staff weapons, many of them with *pointillé* (punched) decoration with traces of gilding. These are Italian in character, and it is known that Henry purchased supplies of staff weapons in the early years of his reign from Italian merchants such as Leonardo Frescobaldi, Fransiscus Taunell and Francis de Barde. Some were decorated specially, perhaps for Henry's guard. A group of four partizans, broad-bladed spears with small wings at the base of the blade, from this group are decorated on the blades with the

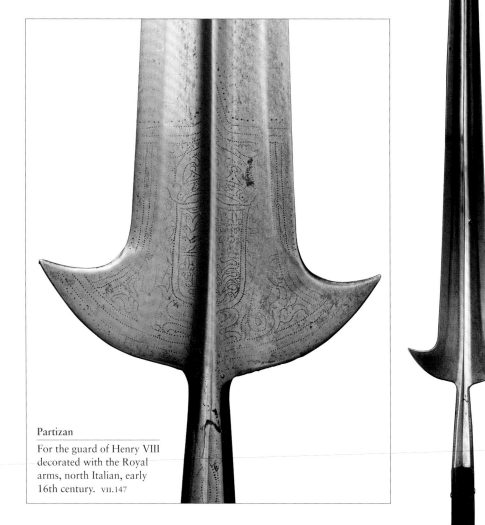

Partizan

For the guard of Henry VIII decorated with the Royal arms, north Italian, early 16th century. VII.147

crowned Tudor Royal Arms, supported by a lion and a dragon. In the 1547 inventory more than 1,500 partizans are recorded, two of them at the Tower 'partie gilte wth the kings arms graven uppon them garnyshed wth grene pasements and fringed wt grene and white silk'. Green and white were the Tudor colours. Also there is a bill with the same type of decoration, but including a cipher of letters spelling HENRI/HENRY. Among the bills in the 1547 inventory are three 'ptely guilte with longe brassell staves garnished with white and grene vellet and Silke'.

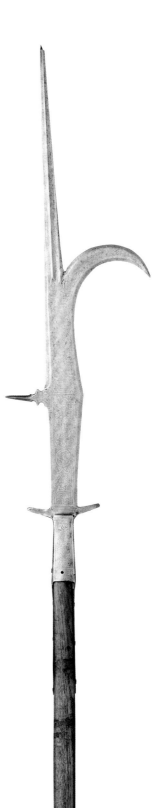

Bill

For the guard of Henry VIII, north Italian, early 16th century, including the HENRI/HENRY cipher in its decoration. VII.1341

There are also 84 'rawcons', which term, transcribed from the Italian for a halberd, *roncone*, may have been used in the inventory for these halberds of the long, slender Italian form, which is quite different from the shorter and broader English form.

Most of these weapons were clearly bought as standard items. Charles V also purchased these items, for a corsèque with the motto of the Emperor Charles V, PLUS ULTRA, survives in the collection of the Rijksmuseum, Amsterdam. The group encompasses most of the known forms of staff weapons of the period. There are two hundred and seventy nine three-grained staves recorded in the 1547 inventory, which probably encompassed what are now termed corsèques, a type of partizan with narrower blade and thinner wings, as well as a variation on the partizan with bat-like wings. Three hundred and six halberds are listed in the 1547 inventory, and a few survive in the collection today, including one recovered from the river Thames. In addition there were many spears of various forms, both for cavalry, called by such names as 'javelyns', 'demy launces' and 'northern staves', and for infantry, principally pikes ('marispikes', otherwise morris or Moorish pikes). Shorter hafted weapons, including maces, were also part of the group.

▲ Head of a halberd

For the guard of Henry VIII, north Italian, early 16th century. VII.1717

▶ Pike

From the arsenal of Henry VIII, north Italian, early 16th century. VII.815

▶ Spear

Right: From the arsenal of Henry VIII, north Italian, early 16th century. VII.47

◀ Three-grained staff (*corsèque*)

Page 46: From the arsenal of Henry VIII, north Italian, early 16th century. VII.1340

▲ Jousting lance

Possibly belonging to Henry VIII. Probably English, early 16th century. VII.551

COMBINATION WEAPONS

Henry's delight in the technological advances in firearms technology extended to his acquisition of a number of combination weapons. One such was a heavy mace with a large spike at the end and three sets of spikes around the head, bored with three short gun barrels in the head. The barrels have swivelling plates covering the muzzles, and were originally fitted with sliding covers to the pans where the priming powder sat. They were designed to be fired by hand-held match-cord, a technique which was standard for all hand firearms until the very end of the 15th century. There were brought from Westminster to the Tower on 7 July 1547, 118 'Great hollywater sprinkells', large maces of this type without guns, as well as seven 'Holly water sprincles wt gonnes in thend' and just one 'Holly water sprincles wt thre gonnes in the Topp', which is the weapon illustrated here. By the 17th century it had acquired the name 'King Henry ye 8ths Walking Staff', and by the 18th century a story had been concocted by warders at the Tower that the King carried it around the Tower at night while checking on the guard. On one occasion he was supposed to have been challenged by one of his constables, who, not recognizing the King, threw him into a cell for carrying a dangerous weapon at night. The unhappy constable feared for his life when later the King's identity was revealed, but instead of punishing him the King is supposed to have rewarded him for his diligence.

Another example of a combination weapon is a long straight-bladed sword of a type called an estoc, whose grip is actually a barrel. The detachable pommel, now missing, doubled as a plug for the muzzle, and there was probably a pan and cover as well. Again the charge must have been ignited by hand-held match-cord. This may be the 'longe Tocke gilte with gonnes having a locke and a skabarde of blac vellut the crosse and pomell guilte' in the Garderobe in the 1547 inventory.

▶ 'Henry VIII's Walking Staff'

Page 49: The holy water sprinkler with three guns. XIV.1

▶ Combined estoc and gun of Henry VIII

XIV.10

In a private ceremony on 28 July 1540, Henry married Catherine Howard. Though the marriage was to be short-lived, and Catherine was executed for infidelity on 13 February 1541/2, it brought about a remarkable change in the King's condition. He is recorded as rising early, hearing Mass at 7 o'clock and riding until 10 every morning, which seems to have had an excellent effect on his health. It is to this period that the King's later armours belong.

ARMOUR

Perhaps the earlier of the two great Greenwich armours made for the King is that formerly in the Tower collection but since 1916 in the Royal Collection at Windsor Castle. This armour has extra pieces only for the tilt, the grandguard, pasguard and manifer, and may have been made for the jousts held on 11 January 1539/40 to celebrate his marriage to Anne of Cleves. It is decorated with etched borders, most probably by Holbein. Erasmus Kyrkenar was the Master Workman at Greenwich responsible for it. We do not know when he took over as master from Martin van Royne, as no lists of the workmen there survive between 1521 and 1540, but in the latter year 'old Martin' was still on the payroll, in second place and with a higher salary than Erasmus, either as a pensioner or some kind of Master Emeritus. An interesting feature of the decoration appears on the sabatons, where the edges of each lame are given a different border, one of which was chosen by the King for the rest of the armour. The armour has been modified during its lifetime, and for this reason has always been regarded as the armour 'all graven and parcell gilt both for the field and tilt' that was modified for the King to wear at Boulogne in 1544. However recent examinations suggest that it was never gilt, and the main recorded modification to the armour for Boulogne was the cutting away of the legs defences for Henry's still-poorly legs. For these reasons, it is probably best identified as the 'Complete harnesse parcell graven with all doble peces longing to the Tylte and the felde' at Greenwich in the 1547 inventory, the only one of the King's decorated armours which is not recorded as gilt in the inventory.

Armour of Henry VIII,

Greenwich, about 1540.

Royal Collection Trust / © Her
Majesty Queen Elizabeth II 2015

THE 1540 ARMOUR

The greatest of the Greenwich garnitures for Henry VIII was certainly made in 1540, for the date is etched in a panel on the collar. It is possible that it was intended for wear at the tournament held during 1–5 May of that year, and is readily identifiable with the 'Complete harness parcell grauen and gilte with all manner of peces of advantage for the felde Tilte Turney and fote' at Greenwich in the 1547 inventory of the King's goods. Not only does the armour have all the requisite extra pieces, but it has a double set of them. In addition it has the only other example of the ventral plate, first seen on the Genouilhac armour. Unfortunately the breastplate for the field, tilt and tourney is lost. The decoration is at least in part by Hans Holbein, for drawings by him of the tritons and other figures, on the grandguard and pasguard are preserved in Basle. The two tournaments of 1540 were the last Henry is known to have staged, but there is no record that he actually participated in them. No doubt his age (he was by this time 49) and great bulk made this inappropriate.

Armour for field and
tournament of King Henry VIII
English, Greenwich, dated
1540. II.8

The date on the gorget of the 1540 armour.

Detail of decoration on one of the grandguards, a triton based on drawings by Hans Holbein.

Arming doublet

None of Henry's original arming doublets survive, and this reconstruction is taken from one in an American museum collection. It is made of layers of quilted fabric, and has mail sleeves sewn to the sleeves of its doublet.

Ventral plate

Worn strapped to the chest to take the weight of the cuirass from the shoulders. It was fitted at the centre with a large bolt which passed through the breastplate and reinforces worn above, to hold everything firmly in position.

▼ **Ventral plate**

Or under breastplate of the 1540 armour. II.8

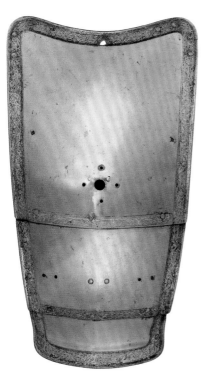

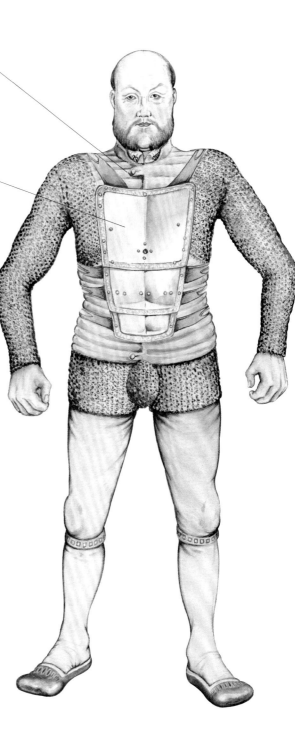

The complete armour for foot combat

Close helmet

The helmet has a bevor protecting the chin and a visor, pierced with sights and breaths, to protect the face, both fastened to the skull by a pivot at either temple.

Reinforcing bevor

This defence was worn over the chin and nape of the helmet, and was originally fitted with gorget plates (these have not survived).

Pauldrons

Shoulder defences of five lames, overlapping upwards (an unusual arrangement characteristic of Greenwich).

Breastplate

With a matching backplate forming the cuirass, fitted with hinged steel shoulder straps and a single articulated waistlame. At the centre is a large hole for the bolt on the under-breastplate.

Codpiece

This groin defence has a central, embossed mainplate with two articulating lames at either side.

Poleyns

Knee defences, riveted to the cuisses, and attached to the upper edge of the greaves by turning pins.

Sabatons

Foot defences of plate. The originals are lost, and these reconstructions are based on a surviving pair from another Greenwich armour of Henry VIII.

Gorget

Fitting most unusually over the cuirass, to which it is attached by pierced studs and turning pins. The provision of the under-breastplate makes the normal function of the gorget, to distribute the weight of the cuirass, unnecessary.

Vambraces

Two pairs of vambraces were provided, one for the foot combat with a series of articulating lames on the inside of the elbow joints, and one without.

Gauntlets

Of the type called mitten gauntlets from their solid plates protecting the fingers. The cuffs are hinged on the outside, and open on the inside where they are fastened by pairs of pierced studs and swivel hooks.

Long tassets

Upper thigh defences formed of lames overlapping downwards, and leathered to a fauld (or skirt) of two lames which was attached to the underside of the waistlame of the breastplate. Used for the foot combat.

Greaves

Lower leg defences, hinged together on the outside of each leg and fastened on the inside by studs and swivel hooks.

The complete armour for tilt

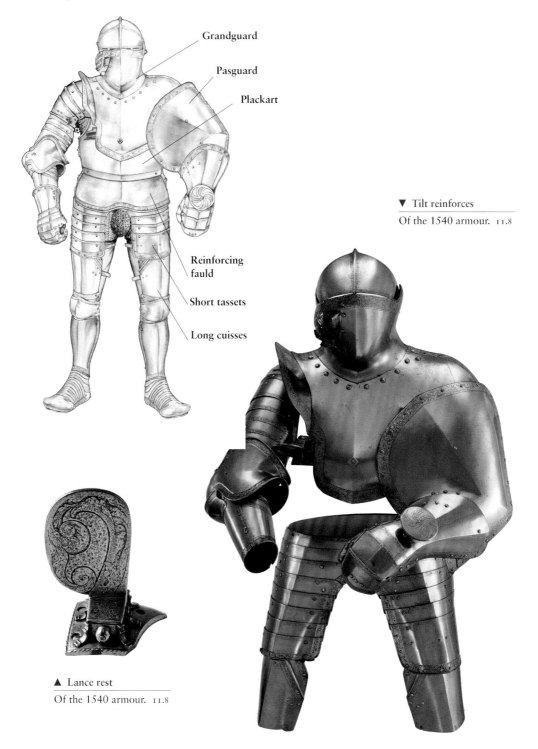

Grandguard

Pasguard

Plackart

Reinforcing
fauld

Short tassets

Long cuisses

▼ Tilt reinforces
Of the 1540 armour. 11.8

▲ Lance rest
Of the 1540 armour. 11.8

The complete armour for tourney

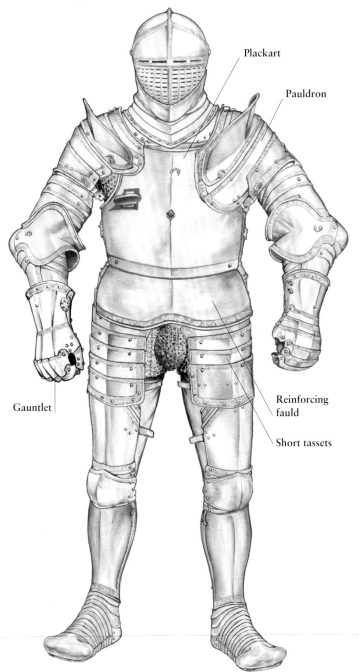

Plackart

Pauldron

Gauntlet

Reinforcing fauld

Short tassets

▼ **Locking gauntlet**

Worn on the right hand for the tourney, this has a finger defence formed of three articulating plates, the end one embossed with fingers and extended to fasten with a pierced stud and swivel hook to the inside of the cuff. The opening at the top and bottom of the hand is shaped to fit the hilt of a sword. II.8

The horseman's complete armour for field

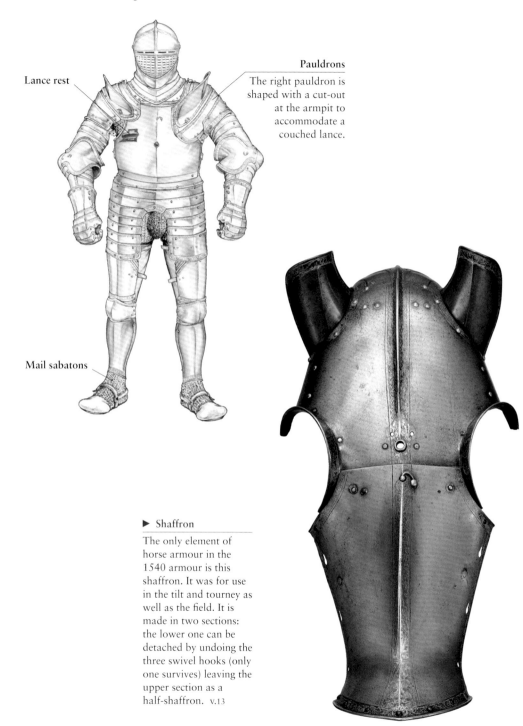

Lance rest

Pauldrons
The right pauldron is shaped with a cut-out at the armpit to accommodate a couched lance.

Mail sabatons

▶ **Shaffron**

The only element of horse armour in the 1540 armour is this shaffron. It was for use in the tilt and tourney as well as the field. It is made in two sections: the lower one can be detached by undoing the three swivel hooks (only one survives) leaving the upper section as a half-shaffron. v.13

EDGED WEAPONS

Henry's new-found youth continued, and on 12 July 1543 he married, for the sixth and last time, Catherine Parr, daughter of Sir Thomas Parr, Henry's Master of the Wards and Controller of the Household. In the following year Henry took part in person in his last campaign, the siege of Boulogne, which fell on 14 September 1544. During his absence, from 7 July until his return on 1 October, Catherine was formally appointed regent.

▼ **King Henry VIII's 'woodknife'**

By Diego de Caias, made in England, about 1544.

Royal Collection Trust/© Her Majesty Queen Elizabeth II 2015

At this time Henry was clearly commissioning weapons as well as armour. Only one of the King's personal swords survives, one of the 'iij long woodknives ij of them of Dego his makinge' of the 1547 inventory, now in the Royal Collection, Windsor. Its blade is decorated with a very accurately depicted scene from the siege of Boulogne, and it is inscribed 'Rejoice Boulogne in the rule of Henry VIII…'. The maker has been identified as Diego de Caias, a Spanish swordsmith who entered Henry's employ in 1543, and was still working for him when he died. The inventory records several swords made by him, tucks, rapiers, arming swords and daggers, and it is probable that one of the daggers is depicted in a portrait of Edward VI as Prince of Wales in 1546, in the Royal Collection.

Another early 16th-century dagger, which most probably belonged to Henry VIII, survives in the Royal Armouries' collection. It is etched with the Tudor rose and the pomegranate of Castile on the blade.

▶ **Dagger**

With etched blade, probably English, about 1510-20, the wooden grip with steel pommel and ferrule 1960. x.39

BOULOGNE

FIELD ARMOUR

Henry had at least two armours made for him in 1544 for the Boulogne campaign. From a field armour made by Erasmus Kyrkenar at Greenwich all that survives is a buffe, the face defence of a burgonet, the standard light field helmet of the period, together with the toe cap of one of the sabatons and the saddle steels. The armour was decorated overall with etched and partially gilt arabesques based on designs by Hans Holbein.

▶ **Buffe**

From a lost armour of Henry VIII, Greenwich, about 1544. II.9

◀ Detail of saddle steel from the same armour. VI.96–7

Saddle steels and toe cap

From a lost armour of
Henry VIII, Greenwich,
about 1544. (The buffe
is shown on page 63).
II.9, VI.96–7

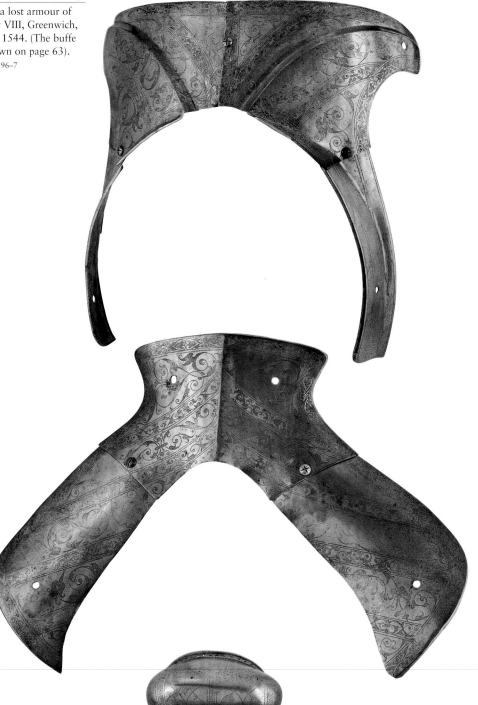

CRINET AND GAUNTLET

The second armour made at Greenwich at this time was decorated with embossed, etched and gilt scales. All that remains of it are the crinet (the defence for the horse's neck), and the right gauntlet. The decoration of this armour includes Tudor roses, on the knuckle plate of the gauntlet. A close helmet from this armour was formerly preserved at the Church of St Botulph at Lullingstone, Kent, but is no longer there. The crinet at least is identifiable in the 1547 inventory at Greenwich, 'as a 'Crenet with Skales percell graven and guilte'. Erasmus Kyrkenar's accounts for 1544/5 record the 'gyldyng of a harnysh made with Skalles for the Kynges maieste with 2 hede pyces', which almost certainly refers to this armour.

Crinet and gauntlet

From a lost armour of
Henry VIII, Greenwich,
about 1544. III.1788, VI.69

SADDLE STEELS

Erasmus Kyrkenar's accounts for 1544/5 also mention the manufacture of a set of four saddle steels for the King, one pair of which is identifiable in the Royal Armouries' collection. Decorated like the field armour by Hans Holbein, they incorporate similar arabesques, this time in narrow etched and gilt bands.

Saddle steels of Henry VIII

Greenwich, about 1544. VI.98–9

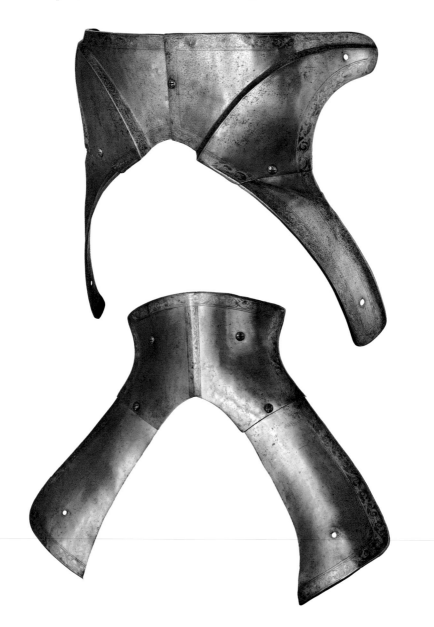

FIELD ARMOUR

Ironically the very last armour to have been made for the King appears to be French. It is a field armour, with a laminated cuirass of the type known as an anime, and is decorated with narrow etched and gilt bands of floral ornament. The armour was preserved in the Pembroke armoury at Wilton House in Somerset, the armoury of which was famously dispersed at auction in the 1920s, and is now in the Metropolitan Museum of Art, New York. The saddle steels seem to have been brought to the Tower with the rest of the contents of the Greenwich workshop in 1644–9. It may be the 'Complete harness of Italion makinge wth Lambes (lames) blacke and pcell guilte for the felde lackinge greves and sabbetters (sabatons)' recorded at Greenwich in the 1547 inventory.

Wilton anime armour of Henry VIII

Italian, about 1545.

The Metropolitan Museum of Art, New York. The Harris Brisbane Dick Fund, 1932. 32.130.7

© 2015 The Metropolitan Museum of Art/Art Resource/ Scala, Florence

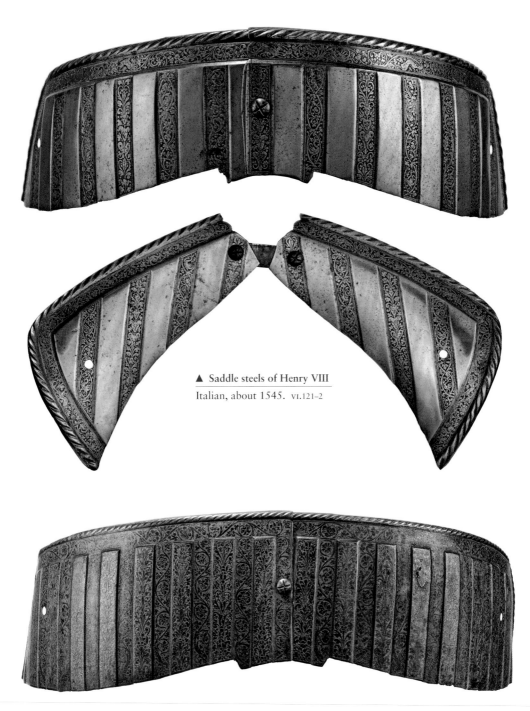

▲ Saddle steels of Henry VIII
Italian, about 1545. VI.121–2

▲ Saddle steel of Henry VIII
Italian, about 1545. VI.114

SADDLE STEELS

Two other saddle steels from Henry's armoury also date from this period. Of the first only one outer plate of the cantle (rear plate) survives. It is of steel, fretted with a design incorporating a wyvern among flowering stems. The whole piece is very finely etched and gilt. It is most probably the 'tree of a Saddell covered with stele plate cutte owte with braunches graven and guilte' recorded at Greenwich in the charge of Erasmus Kyrkenar in the 1547 inventory. The second is represented by two plates from a cantle of three plates. The plates are decorated with alternate raised and lowered bands, etched and gilt overall with scrolling foliage, dolphins and Classical vases. It is possible that these pieces may have formed part of the diplomatic gifts accompanying the negotiations for the peace which was concluded between England and France in 1546.

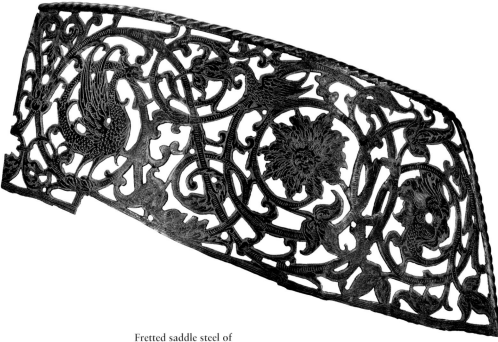

Fretted saddle steel of
Henry VIII

Italian, about 1545. VI.111

SAKER

Artillery continued to be cast for the King in large quantities. The finest of the English guns were cast in London by the brothers John and Robert Owen. An example from the Royal Armouries' collection is a saker (in this case a gun firing a shot weighing 6 pounds, with a bore of 3.75 in.) cast with the inscription 'henricvs octavvs' and the date 1543. It is decorated with a crowned Tudor rose. The Owen brothers shared a gun (and bell) foundry in Houndsditch with Peter Baude from 1529, and by 1536 they were casting guns there and in the King's foundry at Calais. The King took a personal interest in their guns, asking to see a fine double-cannon they had made, and by 1540 they were on the King's payroll, and tenants of the Belfounders House (just outside Aldgate, close to St Botolph's Church).

▼ Bronze 6-pounder saker

By John and Robert Owen, dated 1543.
XIX.894

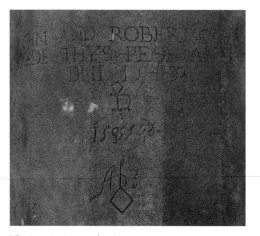

The inscription on the Owen gun.

The Tudor rose on the Owen gun.

BASILISK

The most famous of Henry's artillery pieces was a foreign product, however. It is a bronze basilisk of considerable length (nearly 24 ft / 7 m), and is traditionally (but incorrectly) known as 'Queen Elizabeth's pocket pistol'. It was cast by Jan Tolhuys at Utrecht in Holland and is dated 1544. It bears the arms of Maximilian van Egmont, Count Buren, who was sent by Charles V with a small contingent of Landsknechts to

Arms of Count Buren on the basilisk.

assist Henry in 1544 during the Boulogne campaign. Following the success of the campaign Buren was paid in full and given honours, and in return for this he appears to have presented the King with this magnificent gun. Perhaps because of its size the gift was left at Dover Castle. The Master Gunner of Dover, William Eldred, practiced with it several times between 1613–22, and recorded accurate shooting and ranges up to a mile and a half. It was taken by Parliamentary forces to the siege of Lostwithiel in Cornwall in 1644, where it was lost to the Royalists. After the War it was returned to Dover, and has remained there ever since. Its carriage was made in 1827. As the gun was thought to be a present to Queen Elizabeth I from the States of Holland, the decoration of the carriage included the er monogram and the crowned lion rampant of Holland, together with the head of Philip II of Spain with vipers hissing at it. The edges of the brackets of the carriage were covered with the eponymous basilisks and basilisks' eggs.

▼ 'Queen Elizabeth's pocket pistol'

Bronze 12-pounder basilisk and carriage, cast by Jan Tolhuys, Dutch, Utrecht, dated 1544, carriage made in 1827. XIX.246

TERMINOLOGY OF HORSE ARMOUR AND SADDLE

Mounted knight, from *The Triumph of Maximilian I*, c 1512–19, illustrated by Hans Burgkmair (1473–1531).

© Royal Armouries

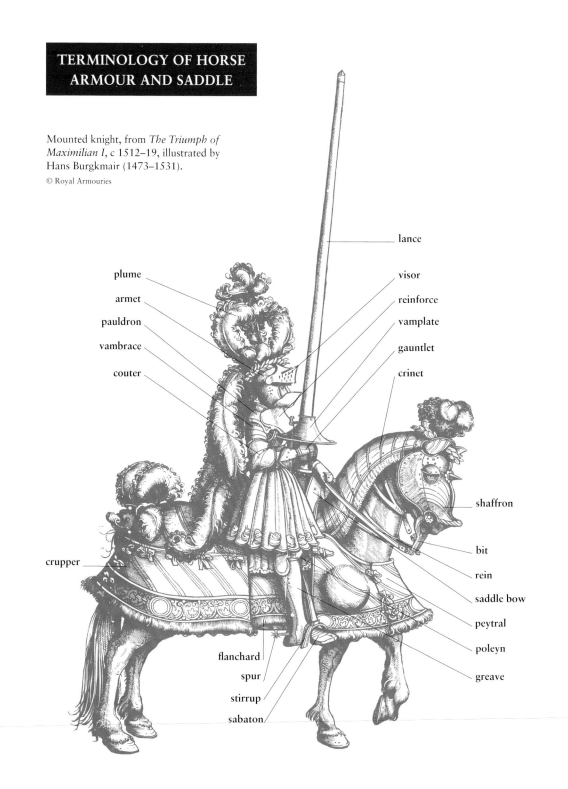

lance

plume

armet

pauldron

vambrace

couter

visor

reinforce

vamplate

gauntlet

crinet

shaffron

bit

rein

saddle bow

peytral

poleyn

greave

crupper

flanchard

spur

stirrup

sabaton

GLOSSARY

anime — Cuirass made with horizontal overlapping articulated plates, popular in the mid-16th century, probably intended to look like the ancient Roman armour we now call the *lorica segmentata*.

armet — Helmet enclosing the whole head, opening with large cheekpieces at either side which fasten at the chin. The term is used indiscriminately with close helmet in contemporary documents, but modern usage is to separate the two types.

arming doublet — Quilted jacket designed for wear under armour, often fitted with mail sleeves and with points for the attachment of armour pieces.

backplate — Solid plate defence for the back, comprises the cuirass with the breastplate.

bard — Or bardings. Collective term for all the pieces making up a complete armour for a horse. Comprising shaffron, crinet, peytral, flanchards and crupper. The more popular lighter bard comprised an open or half shaffron, half crinet and armoured breast band.

basilisk — Large artillery piece with a calibre of around 5 inches firing an iron ball of up to 40lbs.

bevor — Lower face defence worn with an open faced helmet, such as the sallet in the 15th and early 16th century and incorporated into the close helmet in the 16th and early 17th century as the chin defence. In close helmets, often made in two, the upper and lower bevor, both articulated on the same pivots as the visor, sometimes called the lower visor.

bill — Hafted infantry weapon popular in 15th- and 16th-century England based on the agricultural hedging tool. Of varying design but commonly comprising curved hook-like cutting edge, frequently with top and rear spikes. Often termed a 'brown' or 'black' bill.

bore — Measurement of the internal diameter of a firearm, often expressed as fractions of a pound weight (so 12 bore=1 1/3 oz or 37.8 g) Small bore refers to larger bore values, large bore to smaller values.

breastplate — Solid plate defence for the chest, comprises the cuirass with the backplate.

breath — Ventilation holes or slots in the upper bevor or visor of a close helmet or other forms of helmet fully enclosing the head.

broadsword — Broad, flat straight bladed sword, usually double edged, primarily designed for cutting.

brow reinforce — Additional plate often forming part of the visor protecting the upper front of a helmet such as a sallet, close helmet or armet.

buffe — Detachable plate face defence worn with the burgonet in the mid-late 16th century, often articulated in order to fold down (see 'falling buffe').

burgonet — Open-faced helmet of varying forms but characterised by a peak, known as a fall, and hinged cheekpieces, popular in the 16th and early 17th century. Often styled after the helmets of classical antiquity.

butt plate — Solid plate at the rear of the butt of a firearm designed to protect it from possible splintering when struck against a hard surface.

butt — Rear section of the stock of a firearm, held against the chest or rested against the shoulder in the case of long-arms, gripped by the hand in the case of pistols.

barrel — Tubular section of a firearm in which the charge and bullet are placed when loaded.

caliver — Or harquebus, of varying size but relatively short-barrelled, usually small bore matchlock gun held in two hands for discharge, fired from the chest or shoulder. The name possibly derived from the French 'calibre' referring to firearms of specific bores.

cantle	Rear section of a saddle, also 'cantle plate', the steel reinforce for the rear of a saddle.
cheekpieces	Plates attached to the skull of a helmet to protect the cheeks, fastening the helmet closed by joining at the front on an armet and secured under the chin on a burgonet or morion.
close helmet	Helmet enclosing the whole head, opening with a visor and one or two bevors pivoted on the same pivots at either side of the skull. The term is used indiscriminately with armet, but modern usage is to separate the two types.
collar	Throat and upper chest defence, formed of front and rear main plates and usually three narrow lames above for the neck, articulated to allow movement. Also 'gorget.
comb morion	Open-faced helmet with a brim usually swept upwards at the front and rear, the skull expanded into a broad comb or crest along the centre line.
corslet	Half-armour for infantry service in the mid-late 16th century typically comprising back, breast, tassets, pauldrons, vambraces and helmet. By the end of the 16th century much of this equipment had been reduced.
corseque	Hafted infantry weapon comprising a two-edged tapering triangular shaped blade, or narrow spike with upturned side wings. Sometimes also known as a 'chauve-souris', the French for 'bat' to describe the developed form with cusped side-blades in the form of bat wings.
couter	Plate defence for the elbow, forms the vambraces along with the upper and lower cannons of the vambraces.
crinet	Articulated lames protecting the horse's neck, crest and mane forming part of a full bard, or simply crest and mane as part of light horse armour. Regarding full bard those of the neck joining the peytral. Hinged together and closed with pierced studs and hooks, or turning pins and keyhole slots. As light horse armour, held in place with straps fastened around the neck.

crupper	Part of the bard designed to protect a horse's hindquarters. Comprised of three plates riveted or hinged together incorporating an upper tail guard. Otherwise a strap running along the spine to the tail.
cuirass	Defence for the chest formed of back and breastplate.
cuisse	Defence of plate for the lower thigh, articulated to the poleyn and strapped to the leg.
demi-lance	Cavalryman in three-quarter or half-armour, armed with a sword and light lance. Also used of an armour for such a cavalryman.
embossing	Mechanical process in which a design is beaten into metal which has been placed on a pliable anvil of pitch, sand-filled cushion or wood resulting in raised and/or sunken areas.
engraving	Mechanical process in which a chisel or pointed tool such as a burin is used to create an incised design. Technically difficult and usually confined to small areas.
etching	Chemical process in which a corrosive solution such as sulphuric acid is used to remove metallic material not protected by an applied resist of wax or oil paint. A highly popular decorative technique used on both arms and armour.
extra pieces	Additional components for an armour, decorated en suite with it, enabling it to be configured for different tournament events and battlefield roles. Also 'pieces of exchange' or 'exchange pieces'.
falling buffe	Face defence worn with the burgonet in the mid-late 16th century, articulated in order to fold down (see 'buffe').
fauld	Articulated lames below a breastplate forming a short skirt, to which the tassets are attached.
flanchard	Modern term for the plate armour used to protect a horse's flanks. Hung on each side from the saddle, reaching down to the underbelly.
garniture	Modern term for an armour provided with extra pieces enabling it to be configured for different

	tournament events and battlefield roles. Also applied to a sword, dagger, sheath, scabbard and sword-hanger considered together. All decorated *en-suite*.
gauntlet	Plate defence for the hand, composed of a solid tubular cuff, articulated metacarpal lames covering the rear of the hand, either formed as a fingered gauntlet, with finger and thumb defences of iron scales riveted to leathers, or as a mitten gauntlet with articulated plates covering the fingers.
gorget	Throat and upper chest defence, formed of front and rear main plates and usually three narrow lames above for the neck, articulated to allow movement. Also 'collar'.
grandguard	Reinforcing plate for the tilt, shaped to cover the left shoulder and upper arm, left front of the helmet and left side of the breast. Evolved in the early 16th century from the shield.
great bacinet	Form of helmet popular on the battlefield in the early 15th century, survived into the early 16th century for use in the foot combat. Formed of a deep skull extending over the shoulders, a matching deep plate bevor reaching down to the breastplate to which it was sometimes strapped and a large visor for the face; in the early 15th century only the visor was pivoted, but the late 15th century both bevor and visor were articulated by the same pivots at either side of the skull.
great helm	Form of helmet popular on the battlefield in the 13th and 14th centuries, survived into the early 16th century for use in the tilt. By the late 15th century, very similar to and often called a great bacinet. Formed of a deep skull extending over the shoulders, a matching deep plate bevor combined with a visor for the face, swept forward at the sight which is usually stepped, pivoted at either side of the skull.
greave	Plate defence for the lower leg, often made in one with the 'sabaton', usually joined by turning pins and studs to the 'poleyn'.

half shaffron	Plate defence for the upper part of a horse's head. Often spelt 'chanfron' and other similar spellings.
harquebus	Otherwise known as an 'arquebus', 'hackbut,' 'hagbush' or caliver, short-barrelled, usually small bore gun held in two hands for discharge, fired from the chest or shoulder.
halberd	Hafted infantry weapon comprising a cleaver-like axe blade, rear spike and from the late 15th century a broad stiff top spike. From the German 'Halm' a staff and 'Barte' an axe.
jack of plates	Quilted doublet inside which small square iron plates were sewn, occasionally provided with sleeves also protected with plates. Popular for sea service in mid-late 16th century England.
joust	Single combat on horses using lances.
lance	A horseman's spear or the cavalry armed with such spears, equipped with full armour.
landsknecht	South German mercenary soldier of the late 15th and 16th centuries. Literally meaning 'servant of the country'. Widespread employment in European armies including that of Henry VIII in 1513 and 1544.
lock	The ignition mechanism of a firearm, see 'matchlock,' 'wheelloock' and 'snaphance'.
locking gauntlet	Plate mitten gauntlet for the right hand used in the tourney in the mid 16th century, designed with extended finger plates allowing them to be fastened to the cuff at the inside of the wrist, securing a sword in the hand so it cannot be dropped.
longbow	Bow usually made of yew wood, about 6 ft (1.8 m.) in length, used especially by English archers of the 14th–16th centuries.
mail sleeves	Arm defences made of mail, often sewn to an arming doublet, worn under plate vambraces to protect the gaps or as independent defences.
manifer	Reinforce for the left hand for the tilt, worn over the vambraces and gauntlet, and with the 'pasguard' and grandguard' to provide additional protection in the tilt for the left side of the body.

matchlock	Ignition system for firearms using smouldering match cord held in a pivoted serpentine, lowered by activated the trigger into the priming powder in the pan of a gun.
morion	Open-faced helmet with a brim usually swept upwards at the front and rear, and termed a 'Spanish' morion or a 'comb' morion, or with a flat brim and sometimes called a 'cabasset', though these were also called 'Spanish' morions in 16th century England.
musket	Long-barrelled, usually large bore gun held in two hands for discharge, fired from the chest or shoulder with weight of the barrel usually supported by a musket rest.
partizan	Hafted cut and thrust infantry weapon consisting of a tapering two-edged triangular shaped blade with two projecting flukes at the base. Often used to equip bodyguards such as those of Henry VIII. From the mid-16th century also carried by officers as a badge of rank.
pasguard	Reinforce for the elbow for the tilt, worn over the vambraces and fastened to the couter, with the 'manifer and grandguard' to provide additional protection in the tilt for the left side of the body.
pauldron	Plate defence for the shoulder, usually formed of a main plate with articulating plates above and below, usually manufactured with a cut-out for the lance at the armpit of the right pauldrons.
petronel	Small harquebus, short-barrelled, small bore gun with sharply curving stock either held in two hands for discharge, fired from the chest or shoulder, or held in one hand as a large pistol.
peytral	Armour for a horse's chest, sometimes of three plates or one single curving plate reaching to the horse's flanks. Slung around the neck and withers by means of a strap.
pike	Long spear used by infantry in the 14th–17th centuries, held in two hands, often 3.5 m. in length. Pikes were introduced into the English army in the 1540s.

rondache	Circular shield, used by some infantrymen, usually of all-steel construction, also called a buckler, targe or target.
plackart	Reinforcing breastplate attached to the breastplate by pierced studs and turning pins, worn for tourney or heavy battlefield use.
poleyn	Plate defence for the knee, usually made with a heart-shaped wing at the outside to protect the tendons of the knee joint, articulated by lames to the 'cuisse', and attached to the greave by studs and turning pins.
pollaxe	Long-hafted axe with offset by a straight or curved fluke or flat ridged hammer, with a spike at the top. Used on the battlefield by men-at-arms in the 14th and 15th centuries, and used in the foot combat and by some bodyguards in the 16th century and later. Derived from 'poll', a head rather than 'pole', a length of wood.
priming powder	Fine gunpowder placed in to pan of a firearm, connected by the touchhole to the main charge of gunpowder inside the barrel.
sabaton	Plate defence for the foot, formed of articulated lames riveted at either side and with internal leathers at the centre, of ten lames combined with articulated defences for the ankle and permanently joined to greaves.
saddle bow	Front section of a saddle, also 'bow plate', the steel reinforce for the front of a saddle.
saddle steels	Set of plates from the front and rear of a saddle, see 'saddle bow' and 'cantle'
shaffron	Plate defence for the head of a horse.
sight	Vision slit in the visor of a close helmet armet or other form of helmet fully enclosing the head.
snaphance	Otherwise known as a snaphaunce or snap-lock. Ignition system developed in the mid-16th century for firearms using a flint held in the jaws of a spring-loaded cock or frizzen and released by the trigger to strike sparks from a pivoted steel to ignite the priming powder in the pan of a gun.

stock	Wooden part of a firearm providing a bed for the barrel and lock, including the butt which enables the gun to be conveniently held for firing.
tasset	Plate defence for the upper thigh, usually attached by straps and buckles or by hasps to the 'fauld' of the 'breastplate'.
toe-caps	Plate defences for the toes. Foot defences formed of mail shoes with plate toe-caps were popular in the mid 16th-century.
tourney	Or tournament, or hastilude. Strictly a mass combat of knights but embraces a wide range of martial displays.
vambrace	Plate defence for the arm, comprising upper and lower cannons and 'couter' at the elbow. The term rerebraces for the upper cannon of the vambraces and vambraces for the lower cannon were in common usage in the 14th century, but by the 16th the word vambraces was used for the whole defence.

vamplate	Circular plate attached in front of the grip of a lance for the tilt, providing extra protection for the right hand.
visor	Plate defence for the face in many forms of helmet, especially the 'armet' and 'close helmet'. The terms upper and lower visor are sometimes used for the visor and upper bevor of a close helmet.
wheel-cover	Part of the lock mechanism of a wheellock, plate fitting over the rotating wheel to protect it, often decorated.
wheellock	Ignition system for firearms using a spring-loaded grooved wheel which when released by the trigger spins against a piece of iron pyrites held in a pivoted cock creating sparks to ignite the priming powder in the pan of a gun.
wrapper	Plate reinforce for a helmet fully enclosing the head, particularly the armet, which has a vulnerable point where the cheekpieces join at the front of the chin. Used in the tourney in the 16th century, also on the battlefield in the 15th century.

FURTHER READING

Beard, C 1934 'An unrecorded Greenwich armour', *Connoisseur* 93.389, January: 39–44

Blair, C 1958 '*European armour*'. London

Blair, C 1962 '*European and American arms c. 1100–1850*'. London

Blair, C 1965 'The Emperor Maximilian's gift of armour to King Henry VIII and the silvered and engraved armour at the Tower of London', *Archaeologia* 99: 1–52

Blair, C 1974 'Comments on Dr Borg's "Horned helmet' *Journal of the Arms and Armour Society* 8.2: 138–85

Blair, C 1985 Greenwich armour. *Transactions of the Greenwich and Lewisham Antiquarian Society* 10: 6–11

Blair, C 1995 King Henry VIII's tonlet armour. *Journal of the Arms and Armour Society* xv.2: 85–108

Blair, C and SW Pyhrr 2003 'The Wilton "Montmorency" armour: an Italian armour for Henry VIII', *Metropolitan Museum Journal* 38: 95–144

Borg, A 1976 'Two studies in the history of the Tower Armouries. 1: Heads and horses from the Line of Kings'. *Archaeologia* 105: 317–32

Cripps-Day, F H 1934, *Fragmenta Armamentaria. 1, An introduction to the study of Greenwich armour*. London

Dillon, H A 1888 'Armour at the Tower, Westminster and Greenwich in 1547', *Archaeologia* LI: 219–80

Dillon, H A 1905 *An Almain armourer's album: selections from an original MS in the Victoria and Albert Museum, South Kensington*. London

Dufty, A R and W Reid 1968, *European armour in the Tower of London*, London

Eaves, I 1989, 'On the remains of a jack of plate excavated from Beeston Castle in Cheshire', *The Journal of The Arms and Armour Society*, XIII.2, September: 81–154

Eaves, I D D 1993 'The tournament armours of King Henry VIII of England', *Livrustkammaren*: 2–45

Grancsay, S V 1937 *The armor of Galiot de Genouilhac*, New York, Metropolitan Museum of Art

Innsbruck 1954 *Die Innsbrucker Plattnerkunst*, Innsbruck, Tiroler Landesmusem

Mann, J G (ed) 1951 *Exhibition of armour made in the royal Workshops at Greenwich*, London

Mann, J G 1932 'Two helmets at St Botolph's Church, Lullingstone', *The Antiquaries Journal* XII: 136–45

Norman, A V B 1980 *The rapier and the small sword 1460–1820.* London

Rimer, G, T Richardson and **J P D Cooper** 2009 *Henry VIII, arms and the man 1509–2009*, Leeds

Rimer, G 2001 *Wheellock firearms of the Royal Armouries*, Leeds

Rimer, G 2014 'The Horned Helmet of Henry VIII: a famous enigma', in East Meets West, ed. T Richardson, Leeds: 40–64

Starkey, D 1991 *Henry VIII, a European Court in England.* London, National Maritime Museum

Williams, A and **A de Reuck** 1995 *The Royal Armoury at Greenwich, 1515–1649: a history of its technology.* London

The right of Thom Richardson to be identified as the author of this work has been asserted in accordance with the Copyright Designs and Patents Act 1988.

Series Editor: Martyn Lawrence
Series Designer: Geraldine Mead
Series Photographer: Gary Ombler, Rod Joyce

Acknowledgements: Thanks to Gary Ombler for new photography, to Chris Streek for organising the images, and to all my colleagues for help with the work that enabled this publication over the years, especially Ian Eaves, Debbie Wurr, Geraldine Mead, Alison Watson and Keith Dowen.

Royal Armouries Museum, Armouries Drive, Leeds LS10 1LT

ISBN 978-0-948092-72-5

Printed in UK by W&G Baird